To Dylan

Table of Contents

Contents

Introduction

Have you always contemplated starting a business because your idea is not innovative enough, or lack of resources, or too much competition? Is your aspiration to turn your passion and hobby into a profitable business? Are you a creative entrepreneur with ambition to create something unique, valuable & profitable? Do you love watches and dream of having your own watch brand? If you answered Yes to all or any of these questions, then this book is a good start. By no means this book guarantees success, but what it does guarantee is equipping you with the valuable information and positioning you in a better position to become successful! Learn all the trade secrets directly from the source how to launch and operate a Watch Company with great success.

You will hear a lot: "This industry is very competitive. This business is very hard to break into. This is too risky." At the end of the day, you will hear such things from people who are afraid of doing something on their own and they are comforting themselves by asking others such debilitating questions. No business is easy. No industry is less competitive than the other. Competition is everywhere. The most successful entrepreneurs do not concern themselves with the competition, but rather develop their own strategies and let competition study and copy them.

In this book, ultimately, I share with you the Secret Sauce and How to Use it! You would ask 'Why'? Well, simply because when I was doing my research and wanted to launch my first watch collection I had wished that there was someone to share this information with me, let alone have a material like this. I am a strong believer in spreading the wealth, and knowledge is the ultimate wealth to me. If my knowledge helps someone become more successful, then I consider that a far greater success than selling out on my next collection for example. At the end of the day, information in this book will be a great starting point and will help you avoid some of the mistakes that I have made, the rest is up to you and how to use this information to become the ultimate success.

About the Author

So you are probably wondering, who is the author and what makes him qualified to teach us such important and niche book. Very good question. So let me briefly tell you about myself, my experience and qualifications, as well as the motivation behind me deciding to create this book. I am a serial entrepreneur, investor and currently CEO & Chairman of the Board of Directors at AOG Enterprises which holds a portfolio of several watch companies such as Amir Watches, Stranger Watches, Miami Watch Company, as well as other leading brands as El Mostacho Tequila (Distiller of premium Tequila & Spirits), Sana Moda (manufacturer of high end Women's Dress Shirts), and the leading cloud-based social networking platforms in CIS – Moomkin.com. I am also an executive consultant for Fortune 500 companies as part of the AMA-MCE where I consult the executives of top companies on leadership, project management and company growth strategies. All other stuff, you can probably Google.

My passion for motivation, startups and entrepreneurship has led me to an idea of creating a unique book where I would share my knowledge with the aspiring entrepreneurs who want to break into Watch Industry. I am a strong believer in knowledge sharing and I'm confident that spreading your knowledge wealth will only lead to more opportunities and greater network, rather than being afraid of new competition or trying to hold on to your secrets. That's the 10 thousand foot overview about myself. If you have any additional questions, comments or just simply want to say Hello, then drop me a note.

I sincerely hope that you enjoy this book and I look forward to sharing my knowledge and experience with you. Let's get this show on the road!!!

Topics

Let's briefly talk about the Topics that I will cover.

- Watch Industry Overview
- Watch Basics and Components
- Watch Making Process
- Design Process
- Financial Breakdown
- Marketing & Sales Strategy
- Useful Links & Resources

Essentially, I broke down the lectures into a logical sequence, but feel free to jump between the lectures if you wish to. Towards the end of the book you will find a section with all Attachments with documents such as List of Vendors and Suppliers, Useful Websites and Tools.

General Overview

In this section I address the following points:

- Who is this book for?
- What this book is?
- What this book is not?

I've been working on this book for over 6 months, compiling material, recording, editing, screaming, crying, having fun and almost losing my mind, but I had a goal of creating something valuable that others will find useful. Literally, I have almost 50 pages of material that I had to then condense into less than 2 hours of recording. Seriously though, this material is all based on my own experience and I didn't want to use such marketing gimmicks as "How to Launch a Watch Company with 0 Dollars!!" or "How to Get Rich by Creating Watches". No! Anyone who tells you that, is lying. Everything great requires sacrifice. For my first collection, I maxed out all my Credit Cards, borrowed from Family, Friends but I Had a Plan and I believed in it, I was determined. So with this book, what I wanted to do is to put together a series of Lessons that I have learned during my journey to become the Watch Entrepreneur.

This book is for an entrepreneur who is seeking to start a unique business with exponential growth opportunities. This is unique in a sense that the majority of the companies that are launched these days are either reselling something or following mainstream. According to a research, the Global Watch Industry will reach approximately $50B by 2017, with the growth driven by the global demand for fashionable and unique watch models. This book has been designed with You in mind, meaning you as the Entrepreneur who is constantly seeking new ideas and ways to create something unique, valuable and profitable. Essentially, if you are looking to gain insight into a new industry that you know little or nothing about, and your ambition is to create and operate a successful company, then this book is a great start. This material will provide you the key insights into Starting your own watch company, from a perspective of an entrepreneur who is successfully operating the same business, rather than someone who is just looking to make a quick buck by offering a book he just did some research on.

This material is not about the techniques of buying a fancy watch and re-selling it. This book is about launching and successfully operating your own Watch Company, your own Watch Brand. Even if you do not know much about the watchmaking per se, but have a strong passion for business, this book will provide you with the key information on who to work with, how to find them, how to negotiate and create lasting relationships. Best of all, you will learn how to create a unique Watch that thousands of people all around the world will wear with pride on their wrists and commemorate significant events in their lives with Your Product!

This is a unique opportunity because it provides you with the 100% Full flexibility to be in charge of every aspect: Watch Design, Watch Components, Watch Marketing, and everything else that you will need to become the next Rolex. Many years ago, Hans Wilsdorf was in the same position as you are right now in 1905 when he had the vision to launch his own and valuable product that would create a legacy. Everyone starts somewhere. Everything great had always started with an idea.

The time is now and no need to waste it anymore on procrastination.

Watch Industry

History of Watchmaking

The oldest means of determining time is by observing the location of the sun in the sky. When the sun is directly overhead, the time is roughly 12:00 noon. The invention of the mechanical clock in the fourteenth century was a major advancement—it provided a more concise and consistent method of measuring time.

Watchmaking began in Switzerland in the 16th century with the inflow of Protestant craftsmen. A breakthrough in timekeeping came in the late 17th century when the balance spring was invented, which increased the accuracy of a timepiece from several hours to a few minutes. Since then, Swiss watchmakers had launched innovations like self-winding watches, chronographs, or perpetual calendars, and became internationally renowned for the precision, quality, and design of their timepieces, which had carried the "Swiss made" designation since 1880. In the early 20th century, wristwatches used during World War I surpassed traditional pocket models, while the Swiss consolidated their production to weather the Great Depression. By 1945, Swiss craftsmen had reached watchmaking supremacy, with roughly 2,500 watch companies controlling 87.2% of the world's watch production.

Watch industry beyond 2010:

In the global watch market, estimated at 1.2 billion timepieces produced in 2010. Together with iconic luxury brand Rolex and multi-brand watch stables Richemont and LVMH, the Swatch Group was among the leading players in Swiss watchmaking, estimated at 38.9 Swiss Francs billion by retail value. Other Swiss brands such as Patek Philippe or Breitling were relatively small players. Significant non-Swiss watchmakers included

Japan's Seiko and Citizen; Dutch Timex Group, which owned the Timex, Guess, and Valentino brands; and India's Titan Industries.

Watch Industry

As we embark on this journey of horology and watch making, it is important to have at least a high level understanding of the entire industry. Based on this chart, as of 2014, the number of watches sold worldwide has been over 1 billion. There are several industry leaders that account for a good portion of these sales such as the Rolex and Swatch Group.

Mechanical, automatic timepieces dominate the watch market by accounting to approximately 80% of the overall market share, while the Quartz, battery operated watches account to approximately 20%.

Swiss Watch Exports

Here we have some statistics on Swiss Watch Exports for the last year. I'd like to get your attention primarily to the overall numbers as they progress through the years starting in 2009 through 2015, where we see the rising number in Total Units exported between the Mechanical and Quartz watches.

Swiss Watch Exports by Region

Here are some numbers on the Swiss Watch exports by Region. Asia is taking the lead with 12 million Units, most likely Hong Kong takes the majority in this region. Next, Europe is the recipient of the Swiss watches with almost 9 million. Followed by the Americas with roughly 4 million where you have US accounting for approximately 3 million of Swiss Watches.

Total for 2015 we have approximately 25 million units exported by the Swiss.

World Distribution of Swiss Watch Exports

We will not spend too much time on this slide. Here we have a list of top 30 countries where Swiss Watches are being exported to. Hong Kong took the lead in 2015, followed by US and China respectively. The list is ended with Greece.

Countries	Value in millions of CHF			Change in %			
	2015	2014	2013	2015/2014		2015/2013	
				(+)	(-)	(+)	(-)
1. Hong Kong	**2,925.6**	3,808.1	3,775.4		-23.2%		-22.5%
2. USA	**2,195.7**	2,206.6	2,067.2		-0.5%	+6.2%	
3. China	**1,226.8**	1,297.7	1,303.8		-5.5%		-5.9%
4. Italy	**1,221.6**	1,138.4	1,134.5	+7.3%		+7.7%	
5. Japan	**1,209.8**	1,228.6	1,054.4		-1.5%	+14.7%	
6. Germany	**1,145.9**	1,125.6	1,210.8	+1.8%			-5.4%
7. France	**1,136.0**	1,023.0	1,089.7	+11.0%		+4.2%	
8. United Kingdom	**1,057.5**	893.0	872.8	+18.4%		+21.2%	
9. Singapore	**1,028.0**	1,025.3	1,038.1	+0.3%			-1.0%
10. UAE	**846.2**	924.5	848.4		-8.5%		-0.3%
11. South Korea	**584.4**	592.0	496.8		-1.3%	+17.6%	
12. Spain	**450.2**	425.7	384.8	+5.8%		+17.0%	
13. Taiwan	**398.6**	405.2	398.0		-1.6%	+0.1%	
14. Saudi Arabia	**396.7**	361.0	325.8	+9.9%		+21.7%	
15. Austria	**281.4**	241.0	242.3	+16.8%		+16.1%	
16. Thailand	**264.8**	228.8	267.9	+15.7%			-1.1%
17. Netherlands	**222.2**	198.4	184.3	+12.0%		+20.6%	
18. Australia	**193.3**	180.7	167.8	+7.0%		+15.2%	
19. Mexico	**183.2**	188.9	193.1		-3.1%		-5.2%
20. Russia	**172.2**	260.1	261.7		-33.8%		-34.2%
21. Qatar	**158.2**	150.0	139.4	+5.5%		+13.5%	
22. Canada	**137.4**	128.5	112.6	+6.9%		+22.1%	
23. Belgium	**135.2**	136.0	142.1		-0.6%		-4.8%
24. Portugal	**135.1**	131.5	139.5	+2.8%			-3.1%
25. Kuwait	**118.9**	118.9	114.1	+0.0%		+4.3%	
26. India	**110.1**	110.7	117.7		-0.5%		-6.5%
27. Turkey	**109.8**	117.8	121.6		-6.8%		-9.7%
28. Sweden	**93.9**	85.4	68.1	+10.0%		+37.9%	
29. Malaysia	**85.1**	94.8	86.2		-10.1%		-1.3%
30. Greece	**81.5**	84.7	73.2		-3.7%	+11.4%	
Total 30 countries	**18,305.4**	**18,911.0**	**18,431.9**		**-3.2%**		**-0.7%**
Share in %	**92.6%**	92.5%	92.2%	+0.1%		+0.4%	
Total value	**19,772.7**	**20,453.5**	**19,990.1**		**-3.3%**		**-1.1%**

Projections

This is an industry study that was conducted by Deloitte, the big 4 consultancy agency. So what they did is, they completed this survey amongst the consumers in the listed regions (Switzerland, US, France, Italy, China, Japan).

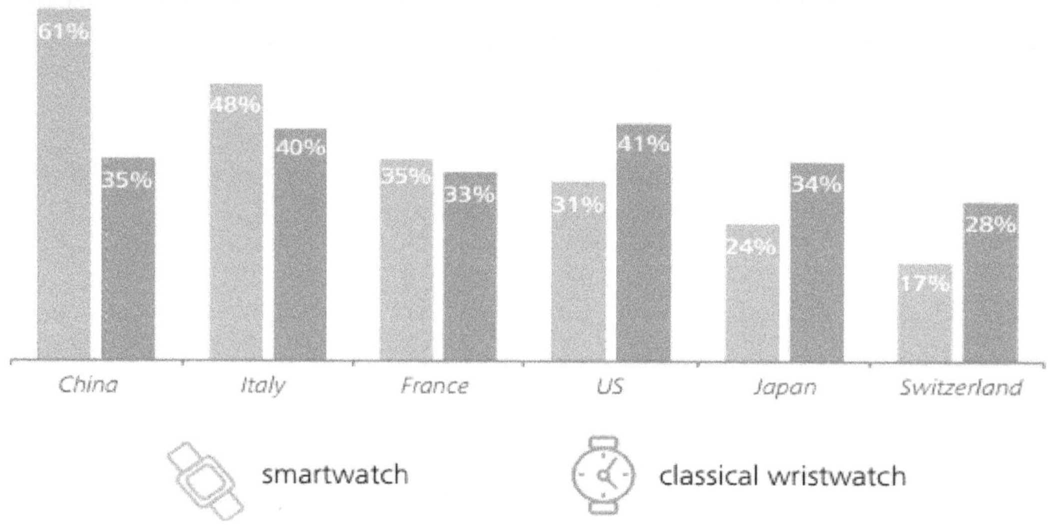

The top chart shows you the Proportion of consumers who are likely to buy a smart watch vs regular wristwatch in the next year. And as you can see there some variations amongst the responses where consumers in China for example are more likely to buy a smart watch soon rather than regular watch. In contrast, US consumers are more leaning towards the standard classical watch over the technology as well as Japan and Swiss consumers.

The bottom graph illustrates the responses to a posted question "Why is it unlikely that you will buy a smart watch in the next year. The top 3 answers were different for each country. For example, US, France, Italy and Japan listed the "Too Expensive" as their top answer, Swiss consumers are not in favor of a smart watch at all (not surprisingly), and Chinese indicated the Smartphone makes the smart watch redundant.

Why is it unlikely that you will buy a smartwatch in the next 12 months? Top 3 answers

Switzerland	US	France	Italy	China	Japan
Not in favour of smartwatches at all	Too expensive	Too expensive	Too expensive	Smartphone makes smartwatch redundant	Too expensive
Too expensive	Not in favour of smartwatches at all	Smartphone makes smartwatch redundant	Smartphone makes smartwatch redundant	Too expensive	Smartphone makes smartwatch redundant
Smartphone makes smartwatch redundant	Smartphone makes smartwatch redundant	Not in favour of smartwatches at all	Not in favour of smartwatches at all	Latest operating systems/ smartphones are required and not all compatible	Not in favour of smartwatches at all

So why am I sharing this information with you, you would ask. Well, we cannot deny smart watches, which are entering the markets very heavily and aggressively, and they are definitely stealing lunch money from a lot of manufacturers who are simply closing their eyes on this trend. But my take on it is that technology is very cyclical and temporary, it comes and goes, whereas wristwatches are more tied to tradition and lifestyle which is here to stay.

Watch Companies Strategies

Another aspect of the study conducted by Deloitte on watch industry is the focus on key strategies that top watch companies have indicated in the survey that they completed. Green is 2015, Blue is 2014 just so that you can see the differences between the year. The top strategy for 2015 was Social Media, which is not surprising at all with the rise of such platforms as Instagram, SnapChat, Periscope to name a few. Collaboration with Bloggers came in as Second. This is an important category because bloggers (especially in watch industry) have strong followership and they can definitely contribute to your marketing strategy if utilized properly. Brand Ambassadors is another section that we will be covering in this material further and it came in fourth place. The rest, such as standard media outlets as print, radio, TV are winding down and the brands are looking to engage with more novel platforms such as SMM for example.

How important are the following elements for your marketing strategy? Please indicate on the scale from 1 to 10, with 1 indicating very low importance and 10 indicating very high importance. Answers only from brands

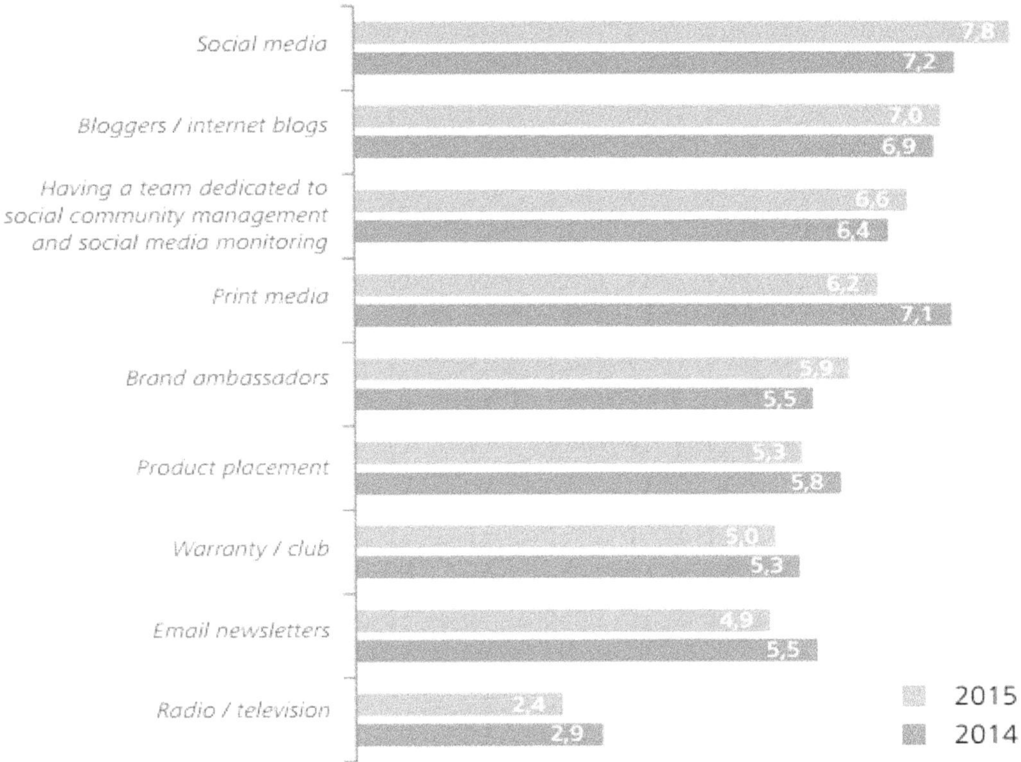

Next, we will be talking about the main players in watch industry, what products and brands that they produce as well as their market positions.

Main Players in the Industry

As the next successful watch entrepreneur, you need to know the key players in your field. The three companies that dominate the watch market are:

- Swatch Group
- Rolex
- Richemont

These companies own and produce some of the world's most famous watch brands. During the next several slides we will examine the portfolio of these groups and compare the various niches that each brand targets.

SWATCH

SWATCH Group includes the list of watch brands that you are well aware of but probably did not know that they all are under a single umbrella. The company divides its portfolio of brands into four subcategories: Basic (the most famous in this category is the Swatch brand which you can find in almost any airport or a mall), Middle (Tissot is the brand associated with the middle category, although there are some fancy versions of it also available), High subcategory includes such brands as Longines and Rado to name a few, Prestige and Luxury are your top shelf with the most recognizable of them all as Omega. Their most prestigious brand is Breguet – a company founded in 1775 by Abraham-Louis Breguet. It is important to note that the company, along with Blancpain and Vacheron Constantin, is one of the oldest surviving watch-making establishments.

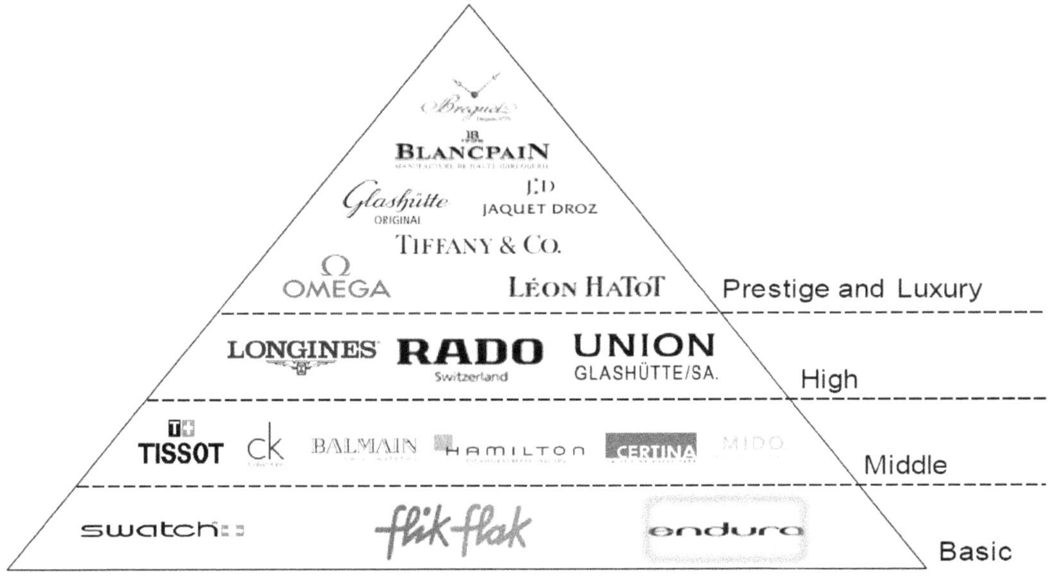

The Swatch Group was formed in 1983 through merger of two Swiss watch manufacturers: ASUAG and SSIH. Formerly SMH Swiss Corporation for Microelectronics and Watchmaking Industries Ltd, the company took its present name in 1998. The

Swatch Group is led by G. Nicolas (Nick) Hayek, Jr., son of the late co-founder and chairman Nicolas Hayek.

ROLEX

Rolex SA and its subsidiary Tudor SA design, manufacture, distribute and service wristwatches sold under the Rolex and Tudor brands. Founded by Alfred Davis and Hans Wilsdorf in London, England in 1905, Rolex moved its base of operations to Geneva, Switzerland in 1919.

Most likely you know Rolex just as an Expensive watch but the company is extremely innovative, with such innovations as:

- The first waterproof wristwatch "Oyster", 1926
- The first wristwatch with an automatically changing date on the dial (Rolex Datejust
- The first wristwatch case waterproof to 100 m (330 ft) (Rolex Oyster Perpetual Submariner
- The first wristwatch to show two time zones at once (Rolex GMT Master
- The first wristwatch with an automatically changing day and date on the dial (Rolex Day-Date
- The first watchmaker to earn chronometer certification for a wristwatch (1910)

Rolex is the largest single luxury watch brand, producing about 2,000 watches per day, with estimated 2012 revenues of US $7.7 billion.

RICHEMONT

Richemont Group is another dominant player with a portfolio of brands, which includes one of my favorites Panerai.

Founded in 1988 by Johann Rupert, Richemont organizes its business activities into four operating divisions: Jewellery Maisons, Specialist Watchmakers, Maison Montblanc and Other Businesses. Cartier and Van Cleef & Arpels constitute the Jewellery Maisons. The Specialist Watchmakers group is composed of A. Lange & Söhne, Baume & Mercier, IWC, Jaeger-LeCoultre, Officine Panerai, Piaget, to name a few and the joint venture with the Ralph Lauren Watch & Jewelry Co. Montblanc is the sole member of the Maison Montblanc. The Other Businesses division includes Alfred Dunhill, Chloé, The Net-a-Porter Group, Peter Millar and Shanghai Tang.

As of November 2012 Richemont SA is the sixth largest corporation by market capitalization in the Swiss Market Index. As of 2014, Richemont is the second-largest luxury goods company in the world after LVMH.

Market Segmentation

Here we can see the Swiss market segmentation by brand, where the brands are categorized by the Affordable and Expensive factors, as well as the Sports and Refined styles.

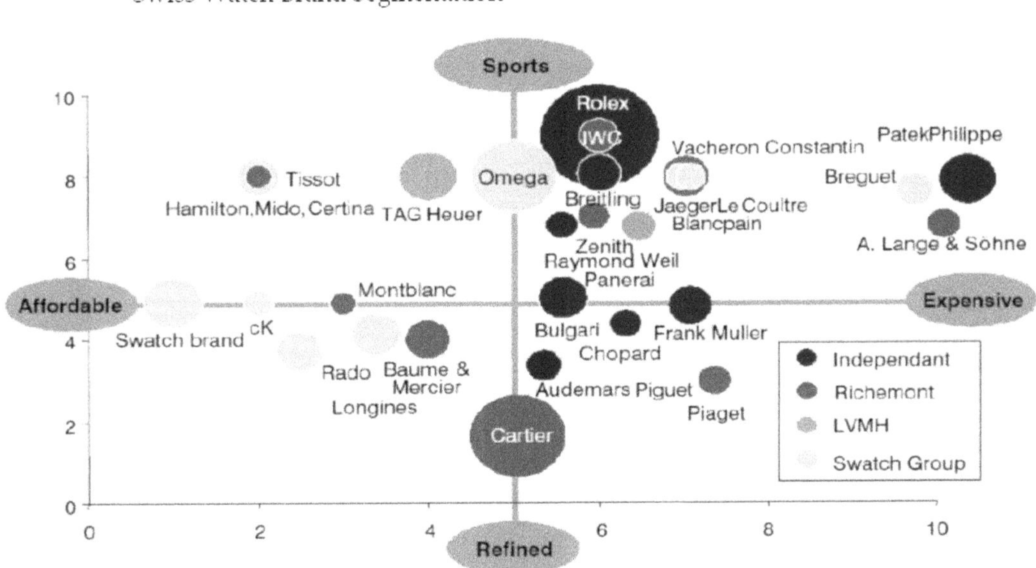

This is pretty obvious and I'm sure you would have guessed it right away, but Rolex dominates the Sports / Expensive segment, with Omega breathing down its neck. Cartier is towards the bottom where it dominates the Refined / Expensive area. Patek Phillipe towards the right, is an obvious leader of the Expensive segment with Breguet right next to it. Speaking of Breguet, let me point out a few things just as some fun facts:

It was founded by Abraham-Louis Breguet in Paris in 1775 and it is currently part of the Swatch Group. In fact, Abraham-Louis Breguet was the inventor of Tourbillon and also produced the first wrist watch in 1810. So there you have it, some history lesson in watch industry.

Watch Market Shares by Brand

Based on this chart, Rolex, Swatch Group and Richemont dominate the market with Swatch Group in a slight lead. LVMH group includes such watch brands as Hublot, Tag Heuer and Zenith to name a few. As part of the "Other" category such brands as Audemars Piguet (which owns approximately 40% stake in Jaeger Le-Coultre).

Comparative Market Shares of Swiss Watchmakers by Export Value

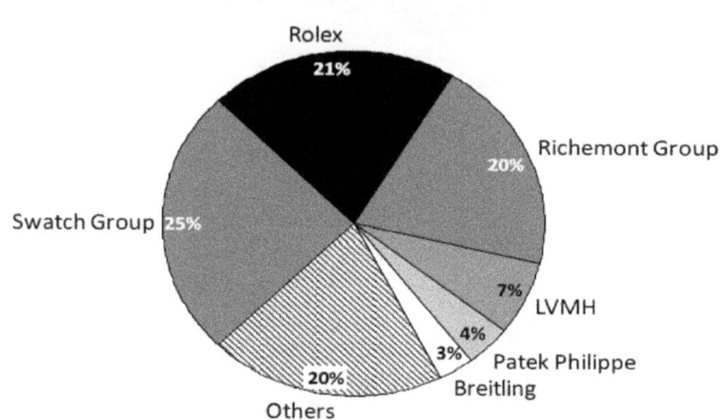

Source: Casewriters, based on Jon Cox and Catherine Rolland, "Watches Sketchbook," Kepler Capital Markets, March 17, 2011, via Thomson Reuters.

So, hopefully at this point you have a general understanding on Watch Industry at large as well as who the main players are and the brands that they produce. Let's summarize this section.

The Top 3 primary watch companies as the industry leaders: Swatch Group, Rolex and Richemont

Lastly, the Industry Numbers: over 1 billion watches sold annually and approximately 80% of the market share belongs to Automatic timepieces.

Watch Manufacturers

Watch Manufacturers

Here are few important items to consider as you embark on this journey.

Extensive research will be your best weapon. Browse the internet, forums such as WatchUSeek (just beware that there are lot of companies there posing as regular members who will make an attempt to sell you their products/service, just ensure to take your time to review). Check out the internet for any complaints or reports on the Company that you are considering. If you cannot find much information on a particular company, then it is probably a red flag but wait till you get to speak with them to make your decision. Also, ask each company that you are considering for few contacts of their clients so that you can get their opinion on them. Those that have nothing to hide and pride themselves on their work will not hide this information from you and should be happy to share. If their customers can vouch for them, then it is a good sign. Remember that they are there to sell you their services and not vice versa, so take your time to ask as many questions as necessary to give you the calculated analysis.

Communication is a huge part of this (unless they are located in the same city as you are, and even then you need to be cautious). The vendor should have open lines of communication via various channels: email, social media, phone, Skype etc. In some cases, you will even get a designated representative or an Account Manager who will work with you from the beginning through the end.

Flexibility is another important aspect. Established and large companies will not be able to offer you much flexibility as they have established guidelines, but smaller vendors can and should be able to work with you. During your initial conversations be sure to talk about the MOQs, pricing flexibility, additional features on the watches and anything else that can help you get started. Your requests should be within reasonable range (for instance: asking for a 100 pcs order to get started and not getting charged for the remaining 200 cases and asking them to keep in stock until you start selling your initial batch is reasonable. Asking the company to make you 20 pcs and keep the rest in stock until you get started is pushing the boundaries of reasonable).

Lastly, the Support System includes such important aspects as Maintenance, Service and Warranty. Examples of questions you should be asking here are: What type of Warranty is included with the watches? How many years? Who covers the shipping charges? What are the terms after the warranty expires? Moreover, great manufacturing companies also provide Marketing Support. Don't count on everything manufacturer to have millions of followers, but at least they should be able to help you with the production of quality imagery for your catalogs and website for example. Lastly, deferred payment plans or another payment plan that will help you offload the need to come up with a large sum upfront. On average you can expect to pay anything between 20-30% as an upfront payment, with the rest due upon completion. But nothing stops you from negotiating.

Watch Manufacturers

As you go through your research for watch manufacturers, you will come across a plethora of companies that you will need to weed out. Moreover, a lot of the watch manufacturers will not even respond to your inquiries simply because of the fact that they are busy and they try to stick to their existing client base. As you can imagine, taking on new customers is not an easy process and requires commitment of time and resources, which is why there is a preference to work with existing clients. But this should not be a reason to get discouraged and you need to continue to plug away. Keep inquiring and someone will start communicating.

Alibaba is a great source for considering the manufacturers from Asia, mostly Chinese companies based out of Shenzhen area (this is the industrial sector and a lot of Chinese manufacturers are based out of that region). Regardless of the stigma, there are Chinese watch companies that produce quality timepieces. They offer more affordable solutions, quick production times, but there are downsides such as communication gaps, higher MOQs (a lot of them will ask you to start with 500 cases and 200 complete watch orders).

During the conversations with the manufacturers it is also ok to take a pause and let it sit for a few days. This will give you some time to think things through and also you will be able to see which of the vendors express their interest with a follow up email which is a good sign.

I am here to help you and not bad mouth anyone, but I just want to also make sure that you don't make the same mistakes as we did, so as far as the companies to avoid, the only company that we have had a bad experience with as a company named SignSTimeMovements which claims to be based out of Netherlands but it is just a single person shop who then refers you to a so-called manufacturer in China. Moreover, there is a middle man from Turkey who will be the filter between your and the person in China. Very complicated. We will not get into the details of a ruined relationship, just the bottom line is a precaution for you to triple check everything if you were to engage with them as we have encountered untruthful statements and unprofessional behavior. Next, we will be going over few important questions to consider.

Tough Questions to Consider

- Does the Manufacturer have strong experience in watch making?
- Is Watch making their primary business?
- Have they created a Watch similar to mine before?
- Do they have references they can provide?
- Do they have a portfolio of watches created?
- Does the Manufacturer have an interest in my success?
- How many clients does the Manufacturer service at a time?
- How is their Communication? Do they follow up? Do they respond timely? Do they provide clear and full information?

These are some of the questions that you should be asking not only your candidates but also yourself. Keep in mind that the Vendor search is a Very long and tough process. It can take months, may be more. Be patient and don't give up because it is an investment and you need to make calculated decisions. Also be prepared to change Manufacturers, don't just settle for one. Keep your options open. If things don't work out with one, then you have other options. Remember, that it is a 2 way interview where both parties should be asking each other questions.

Another important point to consider: does the manufacturer ask you any questions about your experience, about your strategy, about your plans? If not, then it can potentially be a red flag because they may be only interested in "drop ship and be done with it" type of deal.

Associations and Certifications

A lot of serious watch manufacturers belong to certain organizations and associations which are recognized worldwide. Moreover, some hold certain certifications to attest to their standards of quality. As you go through your research, it is a good practice to ask your top candidates if they belong to any of the following associations and or if they hold any certifications. It is not a requirement, but if the response is a No, then you should inquire why is it that they don't consider that and make your judgment from there.

MOQs

Let's talk about the MOQs, Minimum Order Quantities. This is an important topic and there are several points to consider. When I was first starting out, I did not understand the big picture and it has led to miscommunication and certain frustrations when dealing with manufacturers, as well as understanding the general pricing. First, if this is your first project you will want to minimize your risks to the lowest possible, but it is not easy to accomplish. In general, please keep in mind that this is a full blown commitment and no half-assed projects here, if you decided to build a successful watch company with a long legacy behind it, then you need to Go All In. What do I mean by this? I was in the same boat when I first wanted to create my custom watch collection. I was searching for watch manufacturers who will create a small batch for me, like 5-10 watches, something small that would allow me to check their quality and not spend much upfront. In all honesty, I highly doubt that there will be a respectable watch manufacturer who will take on such a small quantity and it would be easier for you to let go of that notion and rather focus on long term. As you start negotiating, focus on such more important items as:

- Can the manufacturer create Free Samples / Prototypes for you if you choose them? The good ones that are confident in their craftsmanship should have no problem with that. In this scenario, you need to negotiate a deal where you will pay for the Production of the Prototypes (but keep in mind that these costs may be high, $200 - $2000 per piece depending on the complexity). Also you will have to cover the costs for creating Molds (mold for watch hands, case etc) but these molds will be yours to keep and can be used for the main production and any future collections. Average turnaround time for creating a Prototype should be around 1 month and the manufacturer should be keeping you up to date on the progress with the photos. In fact, you should agree upfront that the manufacturer to send you photos at every Milestone for review and approval (for example: CAD rendering of the Case Completed and Submitted to Customer for Review, Final 3D Rendering Completed and Submitted to Client for Review, Watch Case is Completed and Photo Submitted to Client for Review, and so on).

- Are they willing to make necessary changes to these Prototypes and if there is a limit to these changes?

- The prototype is technically the exact same version of the watch that will be produced during the mass production. Therefore, if any changes are needed then it's best to bring them up front. In fact, as we will cover during the design process, you should diligently discuss every possible detail during the design phase in order to eliminate any possibility of a needed change once the manufacturer starts making your Samples. Once they start making your samples, be persistent in asking your Account Manager to keep you updated on every step of the process by sending you pictures. Great manufacturers don't shy away from this and make an attempt to keep the client in the loop. For instance, once the mold for the case is completed, they should send you a few photos of that, once the watch hands arrive they should send you a pic or 2. This not only allows you to track the progress but also keep Your own customers engaged. You can use some of these preliminary "in progress" photos to post on Social media, or your Blog, send them to your customers with a caption "Work in Progress. Watch making at its best. We don't just create watches, we create Traditions, and so forth.

- 200-500 MOQ is an industry average. In majority of the instances, the manufacturer will produce 500 Watch Cases (if you are wondering what a case is, we will cover this in the Watch Components section). Then they will order 100-200 watch movements and other components in order to create a complete watch for you. So you can bring this point up during initial negotiations or upon receipt of the initial invoices. This will make you sound like a legitimate watch businessman or a businesswoman. As always, Lower MOQs mean higher prices. One thing to keep in mind and I personally wish I knew that at the beginning is to ask the manufacturer if they have any Watches, Watch Cases or other components In Stock which you may be able to use on your collection which should bring your production costs down.

Warranty and Service

Warranty is your Stamp of Approval. It is your way of saying that 'I am confident in the product that I produce and I can back it with the full service warranty. It is important to decide on the type of warranty that you will provide. Essentially, you need to discuss this with your Manufacturer upfront and agree on the terms. Very good Manufacturers will provide a minimum of 24 months warranty on their products to you at no cost. Moreover, you should also negotiate that the shipping costs are covered as well in the event that you have to mail them the watches. An important point to consider is that you should never have your customers send your watches directly to you manufacturer. Your customers are buying watches from you and expect to have the service provided by you. Therefore, it is a good practice to have the instructions for warranty fulfillment completed by your company. In turn, you will then send the malfunctioned watches to your manufacturer. Malfunctions and bugs happen all the time (of course, if you ordered a 200 Piece Watch Order and 50 of those watches are malfunctioning and are being returned) then obviously you need to go back to the drawing board with your manufacturer to figure out an action plan. But that's a rare occasion. Normally, expect to have approximately 2-3% of your watches to be defected (and those defects will most likely be cosmetic or simple fix issues.

Minimum Service Requirements

Here is an overview of the Basic, Minimum Services Requirements (MSRs) that great watch manufacturers and vendors should provide if not more. But when it comes down to finding the best partner that fits your strategy, look for these Basic elements.

Experience

10+ successful years in Watch making busines

Transparency

From the very beginning to the very end. 100% Transparency in every aspect

All Inclusive Pricing

All expenses and costs are communicated upfront with nothing hidden in between

Low Minimum-Order-Quanities

We understand the risks associated with placing large orders upfront. Thats why we offer flexible & low MOQs

Full Warranty & Guarantee

We offer 24 months Manufacturer's Warranty to cover your product

Lifetime Support

Even after the 24 months of warranty, we offer the best support & maintenance programs for our clients

Flexible Payment System

Starting a new watch collection or any business requires significant startup funds. We understand it & offer flexibility when it comes to getting started

Marketing Support

We understand the watch industry & how to brand your product within. Our team can help design & execute an effective Marketing Strategy

Section Checklist

So this was one of the most important sections of our book and hopefully you took good notes. But don't worry, you can always go back and review it at any time. Here are few summary points from the section:

- Manufacturers: Do your research and take your time!
- MOQs – Minimum Order Quantities
    - What to expect
- Warranty and Service
    - Who covers what and how

Up next is where all the fun begins, because we get to talk about the Watch Components and Specifications!

Watch Components

Watch Specifications

This section covers the meat of this class, the watch specifications and components to keep in mind and consider.

Watch movements is one of the very first things that you need to consider even before you start working on the design of your watch. I have personally made this mistake at the beginning when I jumped right into the design phase. Yes, Design is the most fun part because of the obvious reasons, but you need to stay focused. Why? Several reasons such as movement availability and cost could impact the design significantly. Additionally, jumping straight into design without first researching the availability and the costs of particular movements can lead to unnecessary rework. Yes, you should have some general Design idea in mind so that you can target particular movements based on the functionality you want in them, but avoid the detailed design work at this stage. I would recommend starting with the Japanese Movements (Citizen, Seiko movements) because of their affordability and quality ratio. Yes, nothing beats the prestige of the Swiss movement but you are a novice and there will be plenty of opportunity to go big. Good watch manufacturers have established relationships with the suppliers of various movements and they should be able to relatively quickly provide you with an estimate for a particular movement. Japanese or Russian movements are more affordable and are more accessible. Some Swiss movements such as ETA are also a good start but come with a higher price tag. Once you narrow down your search towards several watch movement types, make sure to obtain quotes from several vendors so that you have something to compare. Be patient and do not let such statements as "We must place the order today or they will not be available for next 10 years!"

or “You need to leave a deposit yesterday otherwise the world will end and all movements will be bought out by the aliens!” It may sound funny but it is true and a lot of the vendors will do that to you in order to lock you in. Once you pay, the ball is in their court, remember that. So take your time! Quality wise, Japanese movements can definitely compete with Swiss, but there are solid Swiss movements that can’t be beat. The other important factor is Marketing. A statement “Our Timepieces are powered by the Swiss Movement” over “Our Timepieces are powered by the Japanese Movement” sounds better, especially to a novice who is just shopping around for a watch. Keep it in mind as well.

Think twice about the Quartz – why do I say this? Because there will be temptation to use something cheap and quick, just like the Quartz movement in your watches, which are very affordable and wide available. To be considered a watch maker, you need to stay disciplined and focus on quality instead of the quick profits. Creating a Quartz watch is just a fashion accessory and then you are creating a whole new type of business, such as garment or accessory trade. You are stamping your name on your product and it must speak quality. Having a quartz watch will not get you the needed reputation in the watch world. On the other hand, it is subjective because it depends on your Business Strategy. Perhaps your strategy is to start from the back end, build up the audience and then improve your portfolio by adding mechanical timepieces because of course they are more expensive to manufacture and produce. Up next, parts of the watch movement.

Movement Parts

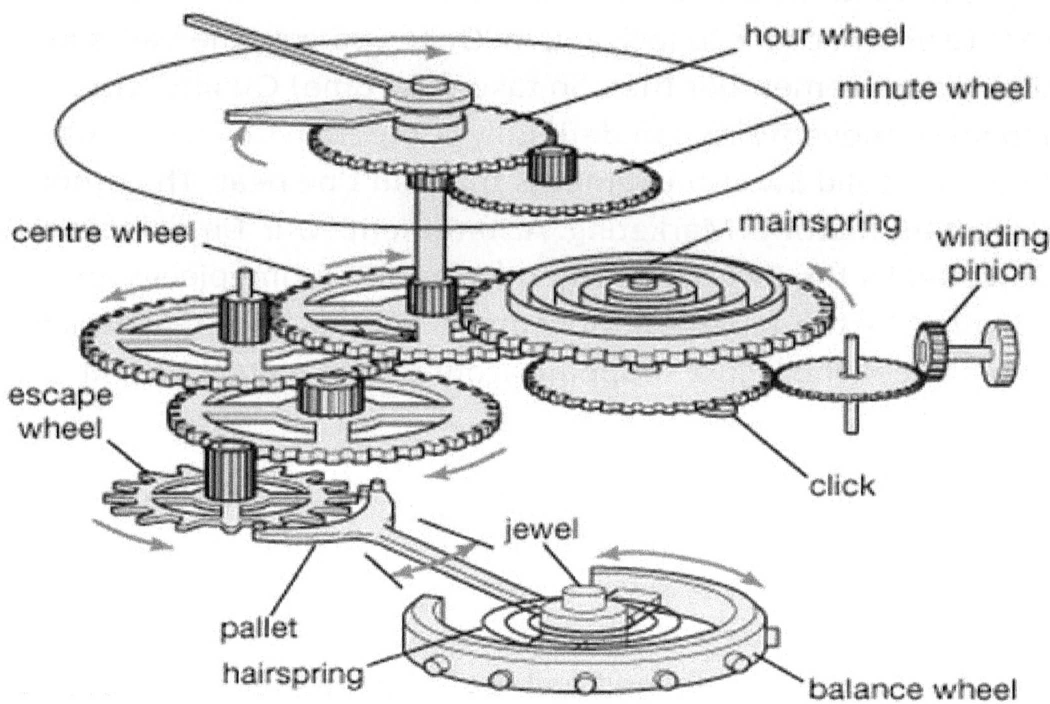

Let me elaborate on a few of these components, if you need detailed explanations of each part then you can easily google it and read more about it. I just want to cover some of the main parts that you should be aware of:

- Balance wheel: one of the core parts, It is a weighted wheel that rotates back and forth, being returned toward its center position by a spiral torsion spring, the balance spring or hairspring. It is driven by the escapement, which transforms the rotating motion of the watch gear train into impulses delivered to the balance wheel. Each swing of the wheel (called a 'tick' or 'beat') allows the gear train to advance a set amount, moving the hands forward.

- Jewels: Jewels serve two purposes in a watch. First, reduced friction can increase accuracy. Friction in the wheel train bearings and the escapement causes slight variations in the impulses applied to the balance wheel, causing variations in the rate of timekeeping. The low, predictable friction of jewel surfaces reduces these variations. Second, they can increase the life of the bearings.

- Mainspring: The *mainspring* powers the watch, a spiral ribbon of spring steel, is inside a cylindrical barrel, with the outer end of the mainspring attached to the barrel. The barrel has gear teeth around the outside that turn the *center wheel* once per hour — this wheel has a shaft that goes through the dial

Basic Components

Some of these may be common sense but still let's take a moment to review:

- Hands (hour, minute, seconds)
- Index (applied indexes or markers on the dial)
- Crown protector (not all watches have them, but worth notating as an available option to protect the crown and it looks cool)
- Crown (also Pushers may be available alongside the Crown)
- Lugs (attachments for your straps/bracelets)
- Bezel (can also be a rotating bezel just like on a lot of divers watches)

- Sub-dial (usually smaller dials on your main Dial to show the Dates, Weekdays, Months etc). On this model, there are 3 subdials
- Case (the core case of the watch)
- Dial (this is your main dial and you can play around with the design of it)
- Strap/Bracelet (depending on the type of your watch. Classy and Dressy watches would have leather straps or bracelets, diver or sporty watches can have rubber bands for example).

Watch Components

The main difference between the 316 and 304 grade steels is the ingredient that fights corrosion. The simple answer is 304 contains 18% chromium and 8% nickel while 316 contains 16% chromium, 10% nickel and 2% molybdenum. The molybdenum is added to help resist corrosion to chlorides (like sea water and de-icing salts). There is no quick visual way of telling the difference between the two. You can't tell just by looking at it. There's no visible difference between two identical pieces of sheet metal, a polished or grained the exact same way. That's why you need a material test report (MTR) of the actual material to validate it as being 304 or 316. Just a fun fact: some tanks are actually made of 316, pretty cool marketing slogan to use: Our Watches are made of the same material as Tanks! For example, Rolex became, in 1985, the first watchmaking brand to use 904L steel, a highly corrosion-resistant alloy that acquires an exceptional sheen when polished. In fact, I don't believe that any other watch brand uses 904L grade, since it is rather expensive and requires special machinery to manufacture.

In general, majority of the watches use the 316 steel, which will definitely hold up better with time. There are other materials that you can take into consideration besides stainless or surgical steel. These are: ceramic dials which are gaining popularity, precious materials, titanium and so forth. I probably would not recommend making the watch from Silver as it is a soft material and scratches show up on it very easily. Again, it depends on your target audience and price points. Up next, I will go over Watch Gaskets and Holders, so don't go too far.

Gaskets

Essentially, Gaskets protect the watch case from water penetration
They provide Resistance to acid, heat, cold, and other chemicals
Gaskets are Available in various materials:

- Teflon
- Nylon
- Silicone
- Others

Additionally, they are Available in various shapes:

- O-ring
- L-ring
- F-ring
- I-ring

Holders

Watch Movement Holder is what keeps the watch movement in place within the watch. There are various types of movement holders, of course the majority of the manufacturers aim for cost cutting and by default they will use the Plastic movement holders. Plastic movement holders work fine but from the longevity standpoint, metal movement holders provide better quality. Be sure to discuss that upfront with your manufacturer on what type are they planning to use and what their recommendations are. Also inquire about the cost differences. Next lecture will focus on additional components that you need to keep in mind such as Glass, crystals and other factors.

Components

Choosing the glass for your watch is an important step. There are few options to choose from, the most popular are the: Sapphire Crystal and Mineral Glass. Although slightly pricier, Sapphire Crystal offers valuable benefits that you should seriously consider when evaluating the components for your watch. It offers significant advantages over Mineral glass in terms of scratch resistance and the overall impact. Paired with Anti-Reflective coating, it will increase the overall value of your final product. Anti-reflective coating offers the benefit of pleasant viewing experience when the watch is exposed to sun, it has a slight blue look to it.

Watch Crystals

There are various materials available for your consideration such as Sapphire, Mineral, and Plastic.
In fact, Various Glass Treatments are available that you can consider:

- AR layer coating (to be covered further)
- Metallization
- Silk screen print
- Diamond Layer Coating (DLC), also applicable to Cases and Dials
- Laser Engraving

Other Components

Additional items to consider are as follows:

- Anti Reflective coating, also known as AR coating is a rather affordable way to increase the value of your watch as well. It should cost approximately up to a $1 per watch. AR Coating adds that slight blue tone to your glass/crystal, and it is especially visible when exposed to Sun. It is great because it does not reflect the sunlight and allows the owner to look at the watch without much effort.

- ATM or Atmospheric Pressure where 1 atmosphere is the normal pressure at sea level. It is a rating for water resistance. So 10 atmospheres means the watch can withstand 10 times the pressure at sea level without allowing water in. This is equivalent to being 100m underwater, but moving water exerts more pressure than still, so you couldn't literally dive to 100 meters with it. Swimming at the surface of a swimming pool could subject a watch to 3 atmospheres of pressure, and jumping or diving in would add more.

- Super Luminova or Super Lum, is based on Luminova pigments, which is a special chemical that based non-radioactive and nontoxic photo luminescent or afterglow pigments for illuminating markings on watch dials, hands and bezels, etc. in the dark. In the past, radium was used until the early 1960s; tritium until the 1998; Luminova between 1998 and early 1999; and Super Luminova and Chroma light since then, and up to today (such famous brands as Rolex began using Chroma light in 2008). You would ask, should I use it on my watch? The answer is: depends on your Design. If you are going for more of a casual/sporty/dive look, then the Super-Luminova is probably a good fit for that particular design. If you are going for a dressy/classy look then it most likely will not be a good fit for that design.

- Crown type: Screw down or Push down. The primary function of screw down crowns is not water resistance, but rather crown and stem protection. The screw down mechanism is designed to act as a guard against impacts or something getting caught on your crown that might pull or damage it while you are underwater. This make since when you consider that a damaged crown and stem can compromise the watch's water resistance and a flooded dive timer could prove dangerous or ultimately fatal to a diver. There are lots of different crown locking mechanisms used on divers, not just screw down crowns. There are flip locks, twist locks, screw able caps, simple crown guards and various others. Some screw down designs do incorporate additional seals in the crown that cap the top of the tube. However these provide additional sealing and are not the primary water resistance mechanism. The primary seals by which depth rating (and overpressure) are tested are the seals inside the crown tube. At this point, you should have a decent understanding about what makes up a watch, basic components and what to consider. Let's summarize key points.

Section Checklist

We've made through a very extensive section on watch specifications and components. Hopefully by now you have a much better understanding of various parts of the watches and different components that come with it. Some Lessons from this section are:

- Take into account Movements before detailed Design
- Swiss vs Japan vs other movements
- Know your basics of Watch Movements
- Differences between Case materials: 316, 304, others
- Type of glass: Sapphire vs Mineral
- Other Watch Upgrades:
    - AR coating
    - Water Resistance
    - Super Lum
    - Crown Types
    - Casebacks

Watch Accessories

Watch Accessories

In this section we will go over an important and often overlooked section: watch accessories. When it comes to watch accessories, the following items should be considered:

Straps: some of the basic ones are Leather, Rubber, and Kevlar for example.

Bracelets

Clasps and Buckles which are available in standard and butterfly

Boxes and packaging: here we will cover the shipping and storage requirements

Engraving, which includes the Casebacks, crown, Strap and Buckles. So let's discuss in more details the straps and buckles.

Straps and Buckles

Straps / bands is an important part which should not be overlooked. First, research the vendors and also don't forget to ask your Watch Manufacturer if they can do the straps for you as well (a lot of watch manufacturers have established relationships with other vendors and can get you a good price/quality). Moreover, if you have your Watch Manufacturer handle your straps, then you probably don't need to worry about the attachment of the Straps which is a labor intensive process.

Samples: ensure to request Free samples. Good strap suppliers already have kits available to send to their clients to show them various straps that they have and allows you to feel the quality of the strap. Do not settle for pictures only, we have made those mistakes ourselves and that had cost us quite much to redo and reorder. Resist the temptation and remain focused. Be sure to request and receive strap samples from multiple vendors so that you have different products to compare. Ask about the warranty that they vendor provides for their straps. Straps is a relatively affordable and very effective accessory that can increase your customer satisfaction, so consider such options as: including a Free extra strap with each purchase, or a lifetime warranty on your straps (this speaks quality and commitment and in return all you have to do is simply replace for a new strap in a case of when the customer requests a new one).

Style matching is important and something to think upfront. Once you receive your watch and strap samples, try them on and see how they look, don't just settle for the standard colors either. Straps significantly change the overall look of the watch so try on different styles.

Customizations: this is where you add your personal touch to the fine details of your product. Small details matter and you need to not overlook this part. Make sure to ask your vendor for recommendations on customization your band or bracelet. They have been doing this for a long time and they can provide sound advice on the best placement of your logo or other customization. Leather straps can have the logos stamped on the inner side, rubber or Kevlar allow for more flexibility with an ability to customize any side.

Labor: strap or bracelet attachment is a very labor intensive process, which requires skill and special tools. You need to have those tools in possession yourself and those are available for very cheap prices on amazon for example, just search for Watch Repair Kit, I will have some links available to you in the Resources section. Watch some YouTube videos on how to change a strap / bracelet yourself. But the point here is that you need to negotiate upfront on who will be doing the main attachment of the straps to your watches (here we are talking volume and quantities and I highly doubt that you would want to sit there with your friends on a Friday night attaching straps). I've actually done that myself, it took me few days but I hated myself for neither negotiating nor thinking about this upfront, so please keep this in mind. In most of the instances, your watch manufacturer should be able to do this for you at no cost, or very minimal cost, just make sure that the strap supplier sends your bands directly to the manufacturer for attachment. This will save you precious time.

Buckles

Quick notes on Buckles: there are many different types but the two most common ones are the Regular and Deployant buckles. For the most part, you will order those from the same supplier who will produce your straps/bracelets. Ensure that they also send you some samples to evaluate.

Regular buckles are more practical and much easier to maintain, they break less and last longer. They are more affordable but have limited space for customization on them.

Deployant buckles cost more but they extend the lifetime of your straps, they are known for adding more value to your watch but at the same time they are more prone to breaks and malfunctions.

Ultimately, the choice is yours and should be based on the final watch that you are building. My recommendation is to start with the regular and then progress into Deployant as it will be give you an experience first with the standard and then add more complexity as you grow and increase your inventory

Casebacks

Caseback is the lid that covers that back of your watch. Casebacks offer great real estate space to get creative. There are different ways to decorate your caseback. It can be solid plate, fully engraved with various markings, such as your Brand name, model numbers, type of movement and other features of your watch. Others prefer to put some laser engraved images. Another way is to showcase your movement (should you have a good movement) by using a "see through" or Skeleton exhibition caseback. You can even use Sapphire on that as well but it probably not that important on the caseback than other front.

Boxes and Packaging

Prior to selecting the vendors, ensure that you have at least some rough sketches or general design proposals about your box. But be cautious at this stage with hiring a designer and investing into creating a full blown 3D design of the box (as it will most likely change after discussing with the manufacturer). Just some rough ideas and 'napkin sketches' will suffice at this point

Selecting Vendors: we have covered few tips in terms of selecting your vendors and one of the first things that you should do is ask your Watch Manufacturer for recommendations, as they already have established relationships with some suppliers, and usually can get you a better deal. If that is not an option, do your research and pay attention to following aspects:

Communication: frequency of response rate and level of detail provided by the supplier. Are they communicating openly and willingly provide you answers to your questions? If you don't feel that you are getting the answers to your initial questions then most likely it will be challenging to continue such interaction especially when you place an order. Good vendors communicate clearly and respond timely.

Information: review the level of information available about the particular vendor. Do they have a website? Do they have a portfolio of completed work? Do they have recommendations and reviews from others?

Samples & Prototypes: does the vendor have samples that they can send to you? Nothing beats the experience of touching and feeling the product and you should be entitled to that. If the vendor does not have samples in stock, then discuss the options of creating a prototype of your Box, negotiate the price. Ensure to discuss such items as: who is paying for shipment, how many changes you can make, what is the policy for handling broken/defected items. These are important and better to be discussed upfront. In most cases, the buyer has to cover all costs but it would be very nice gesture from the vendor to give you a discount or 'meet you half way' should they want to get your business.

Once you have narrowed down your search for the Vendors, it is time to discuss the actual design. Send your proposals to your vendors and ask them for recommendations. They do this for living and can provide you with very practical recommendations on how to improve your design, keep the costs at a minimum without impacting the quality.

Materials of your box: wood, faux wood, plastic, leather etc. are important elements and you should consult with the manufacturer first in terms of costs, availability and how it would impact the overall production.

Practical boxes vs. Decorative: the majority of the watch boxes are just plain square or rectangular boxes with a pillow to hold your watch. Let's face it, once you take the watch out chance are that you will most likely never use this box again, and it will collect dust in your storage. Practical boxes are a great marketing tool which can help you with some branding. What do I mean? For example, for one of the diver collections that we have created for a private client, we decided to take a different angle on the Box and Packaging. Instead of the standard box, we proposed a design of a Leather Wallet with embossed logo in the corner. The Wallet would hold the watch on 1 side and on the other side of the wallet there would be compartments for credit cards, license, pocket to hold cash and coins with a zipper. Sure, it was slightly more expensive but their clients absolutely loved it and in fact these wallets got a lot of use after the fact of opening and taking the watch out. Customers used it as a regular wallet and it had let to more referrals, increased brand awareness and customer satisfaction. This is just one of the examples of how to approach the design of your packaging from practical standpoint over the decoration.

Resist the temptation of adding your Logo all over the box, or making it the main highlight and center of attention. Your logo is only true to your own heart. Customers do not really care, so choose effectively. Carefully position your logo so that it is subtle yet visible, which communicates confidence in your brand and you will not come across as desperate. There are some examples of boxes that feature the Logo of the brand as the center of attention of the box, which can impact the overall experience of opening and handling the watch. Rather make an attempt at adding a relevant design to the box which would fit the overall theme of your watch collection.

The final box will need some kind of an outer packing, for example a carton box that will hold your wooden watch box. Or a velvet fabric pouch that will hold your leather watch wallet. Keep the design of the outer packaging to a minimum, single color and a small logo placement will do just fine.

Lastly, the final customer experience should be considered and tested. Take the customer approach and go through the entire experience of unpacking the watch. Are the items easily accessible? What is the first thing that you want your customer to see? How does your packaging feel in your hands? Is there a certain scent to it? Is there a 'final reveal moment' when the customer gets to the final stage of seeing the watch for the first time and taking it out? Can the watch be easily photographed while still inside the box? These are some of the examples of questions that you should be asking yourself when testing the user experience of your final product.

The appendices section of this book will contain a list of vendors that we, MWC, have been using and still use to help with the manufacturing certain parts or complete packages of our boxes and other accessories.

Section Checklist

So just a quick summary for you guys for this Section. We've covered such important topics as Straps and Bracelets. Make sure to inquire from you watch manufacturer first and then obtain quotes from other vendors. Buckles – we have talked about the 2 types: standard belt buckle and the deployant buckle, which is also known as the Butterfly buckle. Casebacks was also an important topic because it provides various options for customization and improve your overall watch design. Lastly, boxes and packaging is equally important when it comes to the overall customer experience, so do not overlook that.

Financial

Financials

This is an important section because I will provide a high level overview of estimated costs for your reference. This will enable you to establish better negotiation tactics when reviewing the estimates from your vendors. Even though these are just high level estimates, they are still relatively close and your supplier will know that you have at least some level of understanding and can't be robbed in broad day light as they say. So let's take a further look.

Financials: Watch Components

Let's talk about the various costs associated with particular watch components and upgrades.

We have covered Sapphire Crystal before so you should have an understanding of the differences between the Sapphire and Mineral glass. With regards to the costs, as you can see the difference can be substantial, depending on the thickness and the general design of your watch. So choose wisely.

AR coating: some people like it, some don't, and it's not written in stone that watches with AR coating are of a higher value. Yes, it is a nice add on enhancement as it allows one to glance at the watch without squinting in bright sunshine. It also allows you to use it for marketing purposes.

Super Lum is also dependent on a watch design. Sporty and more casual watches are usually heavy on Super Lum. You can use it either on hands on the dial as part of the indexes, or both.

Screw down crowns are a bit more expensive because of its complexity. If you are going for a diver watch for example, then you will have a stronger marketing message with a screw down crown.

- Sapphire Crystal: **from $3 to $25** (price depends on the glass size and thickness)
- Mineral Glass: **from $0.5 to $1**
- Anti-Reflective Coating: **from $0.6 to $1.2**
- 316 Case: **from $10 to $80** (varies around $20)
- 304 Case: **from $9 to $80**
- Adding Super Luminova to Hands: **from $2 to $6**
- Adding Super Luminova to Index: **from $3 to $5**

- Screw down Crown: **from $1 to $2**
- Push / pull Crown: **from $0.5 to $1**

Essentially, this slide provides high level overview on what you can expect when it comes to specific breakdown of various watch components and estimated costs associated with it. This is also available as an attachment in this lecture.

Financials: Watch Movements

For your reference, here I am providing you with general guidance just so that you have at least some starting point in terms of what to expect when it comes to manufacturing pricing. Since movements are the primary component of any watch, majority of your cost will be within that. When I was starting out, I had no contacts and no detailed information on the web, but I always wanted to know some general estimates on the costs of these movements which would give me an idea on approximate estimates. I divide this section into 2 categories: Japanese and Swiss Movement Types and 3 sub categories for each: Simple movement with just basic features, Complicated movement type such as multi-function or chronograph for instance, and of course Quartz, plus Quartz with complications. This is also available as an attachment in this lecture.

- **Japan**
    - Simple Automatic Movement
      from $32
    - Complicated Automatic Movement
      from $280
    - Quartz Movement
      from $3
    - Quartz Chrono Movement
      from $12
- **Swiss**
    - Simple Automatic Movement
      from $150
    - Complicated Automatic Movement
      from $380

- Quartz Movement
  from $8
- Quartz Chrono Movement
  from $25

Financials: EXAMPLE

Here is an Actual Example from a Production Invoice that we issued for a rather complex project where we had to manufacture a Skeleton ladies watch, 38mm case diameter. The client opted for a Japanese Skeleton automatic movement. So this project is more on a complicated side and therefore the costs are higher than average I would say. This came up to $129.65 per model, which is expensive from a production standpoint but it is all relative to the target audience, price points and other factors that go into pricing your watches, which we will cover.

Part	Description	Qty	Price/pcs
Case	Stainless steel case 316L	250	US$22.00
Glass	sapphire crystal		
Crown	stainless steel crown		
Dial	skeleton dial	250	US$5.00
Movement	Japan movement skeleton automatic	250	US$35.00
Strap	genuine leather strap with butterfly buckle	250	US$8.45
Box	All wood, custom Box	300	US$10.50
Hands	H/M/S hand. In blue	250	US$4.00
Case Mold	Mold Fee, 1 time	1	US$500.00
Diamond setting	dimonds setting cost	250	US$42.00
Labor	Assembly / Testing	250	US$3.00
Prototype	1 Complete Sample Watch	1	US$185.00

Financials: EXAMPLE

Here is a sample quote for a Diver watch received from a different Watch Manufacturer. This is a bit more complicated model, as it is a 30ATM diver watch with rotating bezel. This quote provides 2 examples based on Automatic movement and Quartz. You can use these quotes as a reference especially when you negotiate with your manufacturers, and these examples can actually help you compare the received quotes. If the numbers are way far off, then you should bring it up and have the manufacturer provide you with an explanation on why their numbers are much different from the ones that you are familiar with.

Automatic Version		
Case	USD	57.62
Top Sapphire Glass	USD	18.12
Hands	USD	1.71
Dials	USD	11.22
Nylon band + buckle	USD	8.45
Seiko NH35	USD	20.69
Assembly in Hong Kong	USD	9.06
Total Steel Version	**USD**	**126.87**
IP Rose gold plating	USD	11.88
Total Rose gold Version	**USD**	**138.75**
IP Black Plating	USD	11.07
Total IP black Version	**USD**	**137.94**

Quartz Version		
Case	USD	51.58
Top Sapphire Glass	USD	18.12
Hands	USD	1.71
Dials	USD	11.22
Nylon band + buckle	USD	8.45
Ronda 505 far east	USD	4.04
Assembly in Hong Kong	USD	6.04
Total Steel Version	**USD**	**101.16**
IP Rose gold plating	USD	11.88
Total Rose gold Version	**USD**	**113.04**
IP Black Plating	USD	11.07
Total IP black Version	**USD**	**112.23**

Design

Design Process

The design process starts with a simple, raw sketch. This is something that you can draw up, using a notepad, pen/pencil. I actually have a thick artist notepad where I keep all of my hand drawn designs and other inspirations. You do not need to be an artist to do this. Practice and you will get better. The main idea is to communicate some of your creative ideas onto paper which the designer will use as a starting point. Additionally, if you have certain artistic limitations (aka shaky hands), then you can simply use existing images of the watches that you really like, save those images and pinpoint on them what are the different features that you would like to have on your own model. Personally, I use SNAGIT, which is an Extremely User Friendly software which allows you to Edit images, Comment on them, Highlight, and much more. Photoshop is great, but unless you use it on a daily basis then most likely you will either need to take some tutorials, a Udemy class and learn the basics.

These sketches are then transformed into 2 dimensional drawings in a special designer software. These will be more refined and will give you a much clearer picture of what you watch will look like. Lots of changes should be made during this stage, leaving all small details to be added during the next phase, which is a 3D Design. 3D designs will have all the details in the rendering, up to the small tiny design patterns on your crown for example. Be sure to spend as much time sitting on these as it will be much more costly to make changes during the prototypes/samples. Make sure to have your designer create 2D and 3D renderings from every possible angle possible, with Zoom In and Zoom Out formats as well.

Design

This is the most fun part of the entire journey: the design! This is your time to get creative, this is your Salvador Dali time. Everything that you've ever dreamed of will come to life here. In this section, I am not going to tell you how or what to design but I will expose the options that are available at your disposal for consideration.

Some basic design parameters are:

Case, Dial, Hands, Caseback, Accessories and Packaging

In general, think of your motivation behind this watch. What is your motivation? Was it the watch that you Dad had and lost? Is it related to some important event or a milestone? Answering some of these questions will help you get started, but I am assuming that at this point you have some kind of idea of the watch that you want to bring to life.

Case Design

Ok folks. When it comes to designing your case, I would start off with analyzing various watch models that you really like yourself. As Steve Jobs said "good artists copy, great artists steal", although I am not saying that you should straight out just take a Rolex case and use it. What I am saying is use it as a reference point and see what may suit best the design that you are looking for in your watch. Ensure that you take into account various case patters, the position and shape of the Lugs, what type of Bezel, is it 2 step for example. Moreover, do you want to create something that it more casual and sporty which would mean a thicker and rather aggressive style of your case, or a classy elegant watch with a slim case? The decision is yours, and this is your time to shine. Enjoy.

Dial Design

Dials are important because essentially, this is the face of your watch. So take your time with designing the dial. Some of the options for creating a unique dials available but not limited to:

- Enamel
- Etched
- Ceramic
- Pearl Oyster
- Skeleton
- Sand blasted
- Embossed
- Textured
- Luminous
- Cross brushed, patterned
- MOP (Mother of Pearl)

For any of these design proposals, be sure to first get the input from your manufacturer because they can give you an idea of how much that would cost. This would save you a lot of time! We've made this mistake before as we were heads deep into design and neglected to obtain the estimates, upon receipt of which we had to re-consider some of our design ideas because they were simply not the most cost effective solutions for that particular collection.

Dial Design

Few other considerations to keep in mind when designing your dial. There are various options when it comes to indexes, dots, pins which can be Applied, Thick printed, engraved, as well as your Logo. If you dial will have date window for example, consider having a Window Frame. Another important consideration is the display of your numerals. Whether they are Roman, Arabic, or just plain indexes, just ensure to take into consideration your target audience and the overall theme of your watch, because these design elements can make or break your watch.

Caseback Design

Casebacks provide great space for customization on your watch. Whether you are using the full body caseback or the 'skeleton' glass, it provides you with lots of 'real estate' to add your personal touch. When customizing your caseback, focus on the overall theme of your watch (resist the temptation to add something personal, aka your 'girlfriend's initials'). Think in terms of the user: if you were the buyer of this watch, would the proposed design / customization on the caseback appeal to you? General suggestions such as: adding your logo and few technical specifications is a good idea, as they provide some immediate information to your clients about the product.

As far as the Skeleton casebacks (e.g. Sapphire Crystal showcasing the movement) has its advantages and disadvantages. From the Pros perspective: it adds great value to the watch should you choose to add customizations such as your logo on certain parts of the movement (e.g. the Oscillating Rotor on self-winding movements); adding a Frosted Logo on the glass can be a nice touch. The Cons include: limited real estate for customization, extra costs should you choose to use Sapphire Crystal and adds extra room for more maintenance.

Caseback Design

There are several types of casebacks available for you to consider:

- Glass / Full Skeleton, Half skeleton
- Solid
- Welded
- Groove-stamped
- W type grooved
- Fish scale coating

Hands Design

Before you start designing the Hands, I actually recommend obtaining a catalog of hands from your manufacturer or the supplier, most of them have it. This will provide you with the available options that you can choose and narrow down you design ideas.
There are several options that the Hands come available in:

- Straight and smooth lines
- Super Luminova filling
- Sharp edge cuts
- Thick, slim
- Diamond cut hands
- Edges, lines, finishing

Crown Design

Crown is not only an integral part of your watch components but it can impact your design significantly. It can stick out like a sore thumb if you do not consider how it will embed with the rest of the features. I wanted to expose you to various types of crowns that are available for your consideration:

- Water-proof crowns, which can range from 3 – 20 ATM
- There are Custom made crowns which can be used up to 100 ATM
- Push / Pull crown are traditional and majority of the watches come with that type.
- Screw down crown
- Spring crown are also available

Essentially, there are Different Styles and Shapes: onion shape, crown, diamond shapes and many others.

Lastly, some Treatments and coating options you should take into account:

- Sandblast
- Sand polishing
- Gold plating
- PVD (Physical Vapor Deposition)
- DLC (Diamond-Like Carbon) plating
- Mirror polishing

Overall, the crown needs to not only fulfill certain functionality but also be an integral part of your overall design.

Designer

Before you hire a designer, be sure to ask your manufacturer if they provide such service. This may be a good start and most likely, more affordable. Hiring a good designer is an investment and be sure to research various designers. Ensure to ask for samples of their work and portfolio. I've used such services as the Freelancer and Behance and found several really good designers on Behance with whom I still work from time to time. Fiverr is a good starting point but only for the initial sketches, it is definitely more affordable but you get what you pay for. Lastly, with regards to the Fixed Contracts, try to negotiate a fixed price per job completed, or an image or a set of images. This way you do not need to worry about tracking the hours, etc.

So these are some of the important items to keep in mind in terms of Design stage. It is the most creative phase of your watch manufacturing lifecycle, so be sure to enjoy it! And now lest summarize this section.

Section Checklist

In this section, we've talked about the Design stage of your watch manufacturing lifecycle. The design stage includes: case, dial, caseback, hands and crown. Keep in mind few platforms which can provide you with great designer resources.

Manufacturing

Manufacturing Process

In this section we will be going over the Manufacturing Process. I am going to introduce you to various stages of the manufacturing lifecycle. These vary from company to company but for the most part these steps and deliverables overlap and have certain similarities.

Stage	Deliverables	Timeline
1. Idea	Recommendations Discussion	
2. Design	Requirements 3D Renderings Videos	10-15 days
3. Prototype	Watch Sample Box Sample Strap Sample	30 days
4. Production	Order Movements Manufacture Assemble & Test Status Updates	60-90 days
5. Delivery	Packaged Delivered Inspected	10 days
6. Support	Warranty Coverage Maintenance	

So let's start:

Stage 1 is all about the Idea. During this stage the client and the manufacturer discuss different ideas, exchange information and the client provides high level sketches about the type of watch that they want to bring to life. The manufacturer provides recommendations, suggestions on areas for improvement.

Stage 2 is all about the Technical Requirements and the Design. During this phase, the requirements are spelled out as far as what functions and features the client wants in the watch and the manufacturer provides solutions as far as what type of movements are available that will meet those requirements. Once these features are agreed upon, the renderings are put together, which start with basic raw drawings and progress into final 3D professional renderings. Also, some introductory videos can be created during this stage. Typically expect for this phase to be between 10 to 15 days. Also during this 2nd stage the manufacturer provides the estimates and a quote. Once the manufacturer and the client are on the same page with that regard, expect to have a deposit or a prepayment to be made so that the manufacturer can move on to the next phase.

Stage 3 is focused on the Samples or the Prototype. The manufacturer starts working on the Case, hands and Dial moulds, and the final technical specifications document is prepared. During this stage, the client works on Accessories and other important aspects as the Packaging and Straps. Prototype or a Sample typically takes a month to complete (depending on complexity and level of complications in the watch).

Once the Prototype is completed, the manufacturer mails it to the client for review, analysis. Hopefully there are no significant modifications are needed and the client is happy with the output. Once the client approves the prototype and gives the Green light for the Full Production to Start, that is when the **Stage 4** starts which is Production. During the Stage 4, the manufacturer orders the movements, completes the production of bulk components (cases, dials, glass, casebacks, hands etc.). Followed by the assembly and testing. Throughout each stage, the manufacturer should keep the client updated on the progress. Great manufacturers even provide pictures and photos of the progress, that way the client can even use these images in their marketing. Roughly expect for this stage to take between 2 and 3 months. Once the bulk production is completed, passed Quality Assurance and Testing, it is packaged and prepared for shipment to the client. The client receives the packages, inspects.

Throughout all stages, especially after the Prototypes are completed and delivered, the client should focus on creating and executing their Marketing Strategy (which we will cover further) to build Pre-Launch buzz, collect pre orders and position the product for success way in advance before it is even completed.

Manufacturing Process

The manufacturer performs various types of testing during and after completion of the manufacturing process. I wanted you to be at least exposed at high level to various types of testing that is performed.

Water Resistance testing is conducted using special machinery which basically tests the watch for the specified atmospheric pressure.

Drop testing is performed to ensure watch stability and performance when exposed to impact. Some manufacturers have special equipment for that, others perform drop tests by simply dropping the watches from a particular height.

High and Low Temperature testing is done using special equipment to meet certain minimum standards when exposed to particular temperatures.

UV Light and artificial sweat testing are also performed. You should inquire from your manufacturer on the types of testing that they are going to perform as part of the manufacturing process and they should provide you with at least high level explanation on what each type of testing involves.

Marketing

Marketing Strategy

At this point, you should have a good level of understanding on watch industry, design, components and the manufacturing processes. These are essential, but the Marketing Strategy is another half of successful launch and operation of a Watch Company. The next lectures will focus on various methods on how to create and implement a marketing strategy that works and delivers results.

As you think of your watch design and other fun stuff, you need to spend some time asking yourself and answering some tough questions. Agreed, those are not the most fun but it has to be done. It will take some time for you to uncover the answers to some of these questions, so do not rush. A lot of times, new entrepreneurs are in so much love with their products that they tend to be a bit too self-persuasive. What do I mean? I've made that same mistake before, when I thought that I created a watch that the entire world will love. I did not think of any strategy, fully relying on the concept that the great product will sell itself. Well, it does not. Even Rolex requires selling and marketing. Products don't sell themselves, you do. Even if you have the most unique watch design in the world, you still need to get this design in front of the right people and make sure that your target audience is aware that it exists.

The following lectures will focus on the following areas:

- What is your story?
- Who is your customer?
- What is your USP (Unique Selling Proposition)?
- What is your distribution strategy?
- What is your Pricing Strategy?
- What are your marketing channels?

Marketing Strategy: Your Watch Story

Bottom line, people love stories and you need to have a captivating story. These are some of the helpful points to keep in mind when writing your short story. First, the story needs to be brief, do not drag and mention every possible detail, people get bored. Open the story with a strong opening, an attention grabber so to say, if you don't have one, come up with one. Something like "It was Thursday night and I was at the bar of the 4 Seasons, waiting for my meeting. As I was typing up a response on my iPhone, I've noticed an incredibly attractive blonde at the corner of my eye, sitting down at the bar next to me. "Hi there, do you know what time it is?" she asked. I couldn't respond properly as I did not have my watch on. She noticed slight hesitation in my actions and offered to buy me a drink. We shared a toast, and after that first sip, I noticed how things got blurry and next thing I know, I wake up in the bathtub full of ice. The phone, which was lying next to me on a chair, rang and a mysterious voice on the other end whispered: "Do not panic. There is a tube, sticking out of your lower back and you are now a member of an underground Organ Harvesting Operation. Follow our Instructions and you will survive!"

Got your attention right? But not all stories need to be so extreme, you get the point. People also love the good ol' stories of overcoming obstacles and rising from the ash. Think of any challenges that presented themselves as you embarked on this journey to become the next Watch Legacy.

What is your motivation for creating this watch company? Perhaps, your grandfather was an avid watch collector and he passed down one of his grail watches down to you from your father as he survived the World War II and you now want to pay tribute to that legacy by creating your own watch line and naming it something within those lines?

What are some of the sacrifices that you had to make in order to bring this idea to life? Perhaps you had to quit your full time job and go into this business fulltime while working nights and weekends as a waiter.

Do not ignore a good story. There a lot of watches out there. What sets you apart? A good and captivating story can help you achieve that.

Marketing Strategy: Your Customer

Understanding who your customer is an important element of successful launch. Studying and understanding your target group will provide you with a competitive advantage as you cater to those needs. Start small, grow big. Select a small niche group of people that you would want to target first with your initial watch collection. This initial group of people will be your early adopters so select carefully. They will also provide you with the valuable feedback, take it constructively and do not get offended. During my initial launches, I used to get very upset if someone gave me negative feedback about the product or a way we were marketing it. In fact, try to listen to what they are saying as it might provide you with additional ways to improve in the future. Some segmentation can help with narrowing down your scope: for example, if you live in NYC, you can select New Yorkers as your initial target customers which can be narrowed down even further. This will allow you to create a localized marketing strategy that you can execute more effectively "on the ground" rather than trying to conquer the world from the get go.

Let me give you an example. One of our portfolio companies, Amir Watches has a target audience of Kazakhstan. I am from Kazakhstan and my partner in that company is from Kazakhstan, so we know the history and cultural preferences. With that in mind, we decided to create a collection which would pay tribute to deep historical roots of that country, even hired a historian who helped us find an ornament with deep meaning which we incorporated into our design of the first collection. This was accompanied by truthful and intriguing story. At this point, the company is very successful in Central Asia, grossing over half a million dollars in sales in its first year and we are now expanding into neighboring regions with unique collections as such.

Marketing Strategy: Your Product

With regards to the Product: At the end of the day, unless you come from a family of watchmakers with 100 year old history and now you are teaming up with your great-grandfather to create a watch collection, it would be rather difficult to come with something so unique that would stand out of the crowd. Sure, your design may look cool (at least to you and your mom) but you need a creative way to brand your watch collection. Don't go for something like "Revolutionary Design paired with Innovative Technology at affordable price". This doesn't mean anything. Instead, I recommend targeting a small and niche market for whom you can create something special. For example, one of our most successful brands, Amir Watches, is designed specifically for Kazakhstan – market so small (total 17MM population) and we wanted to pay tribute to the depth of that culture with a design that spoke the traditions and ancient history of that country. Pair that with quality ingredients like solid movement and you have yourself a solid start. That stuff sells! Sure you may say, but I don't know anyone in Kazakhstan and there is no way I can travel so far. Just look around yourself, think of what you love and what surrounds you and try to think of a small audience whom you can target and grow from there.

Marketing Strategy: Distribution Channels

Distribution Channels is an integral part of your Marketing Plan. It will help you define your targeted channels for selling your product. Here we need to focus on few avenues: Online, Offline (such as jewelry stores, other boutiques), Direct Sales is what you can explore if you have your own space. And retailers, which can be effective if you choose the right partners. So let me cover this point in more detail further.

Marketing Strategy: Retailers

First, what is consignment? Not everyone is familiar with this concept so let me provide some clarity. **Consignment** is the act of **consigning**, which in turn is the act of giving over to another person or agent's charge, custody or care any material or goods, but retaining legal ownership until the material or goods are sold. This may be done for the purpose of shipping the goods, transferring the goods to auction, or with the intent of the goods being placed on sale in a store (i.e., a **consignment shop**).

The verb "*consign*" means "to send"; and therefore the noun "*consignment*" means "sending goods to another person". In the case of "*retail consignment*" or "*sales consignment*" (often just referred to as a "consignment"), goods are sent to the agent for the purpose of sale. The ownership of these goods remains with the sender. The agent sells the goods on behalf of the sender, according to their instructions. The sender of goods is known as the "*consignor*" and the agent entrusted with the custody and care of the goods is known as the "*consignee*".

Partnering with Retailers and specialty stores is a good idea, for the most part. The primary drawback is of course, they will want substantial discounts and % cuts for sales commission. On the flipside, they are a supplementary income and a marketing channel for your watches. Besides, if you are convincing enough, your watches will be displayed along the lines of already established watch brands, which gives you nothing but the credibility. At the Appendices section of this book, you can download one of the Consignment Agreements that we use, which is your standard document that you should sign with your retailers. In most instances, watch retail and jewelry stores welcome new products and yours will not an exception. They like more variety in their product lines so keep this in mind as you do have some negotiation powers as you discuss the terms with them.

Most likely you are a brand new company and no one has ever heard of you. Keep that in mind and don't get discouraged when some retailers would not get involved with unknown brands, keep looking and you will find the partners that are right for you and your strategy.

Distribution Channels: Online

If you decide that your primary distribution will occur online, then most likely you will be using your website as the main mechanism for sales. I will not make this book on How to Build a Killer Website, as there are plenty of other great books specifically on that topic and I recommend you guys do check them out, but I want to point out few important things to keep in mind as you start building your website.

It needs to be fast loading, with easy navigation. Additionally, Smart Shopping cart with recommendations is almost a standard these days. Quick and seamless check out process is also expected. Social Media accessibility but not too much is also important to allow your customers help you spread the word. Search Engine Optimization is critical to help the search engines easily and quickly scan your website. You should at least understand the basics of keyword analysis, competitor SEO analysis, and worst case hire an SEO specialist whom you can find at affordable rates on Fiverr for example. Blog section allows you to come across as more human and share you stories with the clients. Lastly, Elance/UpWork and Fiverr is a good source to find quality and affordable programmers who can help you build a killer website. Up next, I am going to go over the Pricing strategies for your watches.

Marketing Strategy: Pricing

To develop a pricing strategy, the first step is to gather data:

- Competitor prices and pricing strategies
- Customer perception of products and services
- Customer benefits of products and services
- Cost of producing, procuring, or generating products and services (variable costs)
- Fixed business costs (overhead)

Secondly, you should take into consideration your **Design and Packaging** (I'm sure you know that all expensive things come packaged in really nice boxes). **Availability**: are you creating a limited edition collection which will only be available in 50 timepieces and will never be made again? That will also impact your pricing. **Uniqueness**: how unique is your watch? Perhaps you came up with something that other watches don't have? Or your watches come packaged with a Members Only Club who gets to attend a Private Dinner with Top 10 Watch Manufacturers at the Annual Watch Conference in Basel Switzerland?

Cost Plus: Production costs are determined and then a target profit margin is applied. For example, if a product costs $100 to manufacture, and the business wants to make a 20% profit, the price is $120 per unit.

Lastly, the magic **number 9** sells better than any other number. Prices ending in 9 are more appealing. $499 is better than $500, period. It's a psychology that has worked well for a very long time, so don't underestimate it.

Also, think of strategic pricing in terms of Volume and Margin. Do you want to earn more per unit, or per collection? This will help you determine the pricing of your watches. Next lecture will focus on various Channels to be considered as part of your Marketing Strategy.

Marketing Strategy: Channels

A significant portion of your Marketing Strategy shall be devoted to this section: Your Marketing Channels. This is the meat of your Plan: how will you market your product and how will your target audience find out about it? There is a lot more that can go into this depending on your product, audience, and other parameters, but I wanted for you to be familiar with 4 key aspects: SMM, Crowdfunding, Ambassadors and Reviews. Why? Well, simply because they have worked and continue to work for our watch projects. The next several slides will focus exactly on that.

Marketing Channels: SMM

Again, this class is not about SMM and I will not make an attempt to share all the secrets of effective SMM or how to get 10K Followers on Instagram, but rather I will share some of the strategies that have worked well for us, so that at least you have some foundation for a solid start.

First, you need to analyze the most appropriate platform. For instance, we use Instagram, Facebook, Tumblr and Pinterest. It may seem like a lot, but they encompass various audiences, expand our reach and allow for various means for staying in touch with your audience. Pinterest and Instagram are image oriented platforms and that provides us with additional opportunities to showcase our Designs, Collections and any new ideas that we have in the works.

This does not mean that you should create your profiles on the day of your launch. In fact, you should start your SMM as soon as you finish this book, meaning that you will be ready to bring your watch idea to life. This will allow you to build up a fan base, get input from them and prepare for the big launch.

Marketing Channels: SMM

SMM allows you to reach masses of people but it takes time and persistence to get your message across and get people to notice. For that, you need to develop an actual strategy. SMM is all about engagement, sure you can boost your likes, comments, shares, views, retweets etc, but at the end of the day – will this generate more sales for you?

Some of the few strategies that have worked well for us are: Posting images of upcoming collections and asking for feedback, encouraging feedback and replying to comments. It is important to stay engaged. Some of the larger brands cannot afford to reply to every single comment or a question, but you being a startup should take the time to reply and answer any questions. Posting Polls and Questionnaires is also engaging because it provides your audience with several choices and does not require them to think too much. It also shows your willingness to listen to feedback and comments.

Contests and Giveaways: those work well if you are genuine about it. Post Contest that encourage your audience to share the news about you with their friends. Come up with some creative ways to motivate your fans to help you spread the word. Offer incentives, discounts, perks and then promote your winners to show that you did come through and delivered on the promise.

Active SMM will also require you to Like, Comment, View and engage with others. This does not mean that you should only be concerned about the Posts/Images that you post. You should provide feedback and comments to others.

Marketing Channels: Crowdfunding

Crowdfunding is one of our main sources for expanding our customer base.

Crowdfunding is the practice of funding a project or venture by raising monetary contributions from a large number of people, typically via the internet. Succeeding with Crowdfunding is not easy but it is not rocket science either. Properly executed strategy paired with persistence and creativity will position you towards success. One would ask: why would I want to do Crowdfunding? Isn't it like begging the crowds of people to give you money? Not necessarily. You need a proper plan to do that. There are 2 main platforms for Crowdfunding: KickStarter (which is slightly larger than IGG), and IndieGogo.

Let's spend some time analyzing the Business Case on the actual example of our own Kickstarter campaign for Stranger Watches.

For this section of the book we will actually go through our KickStarter campaign that we launched last year for one of our collections: Stranger Watches.

The actual URL is available:

https://www.kickstarter.com/projects/stranger/stranger-time-thoroughbred-collection-of-watches/description

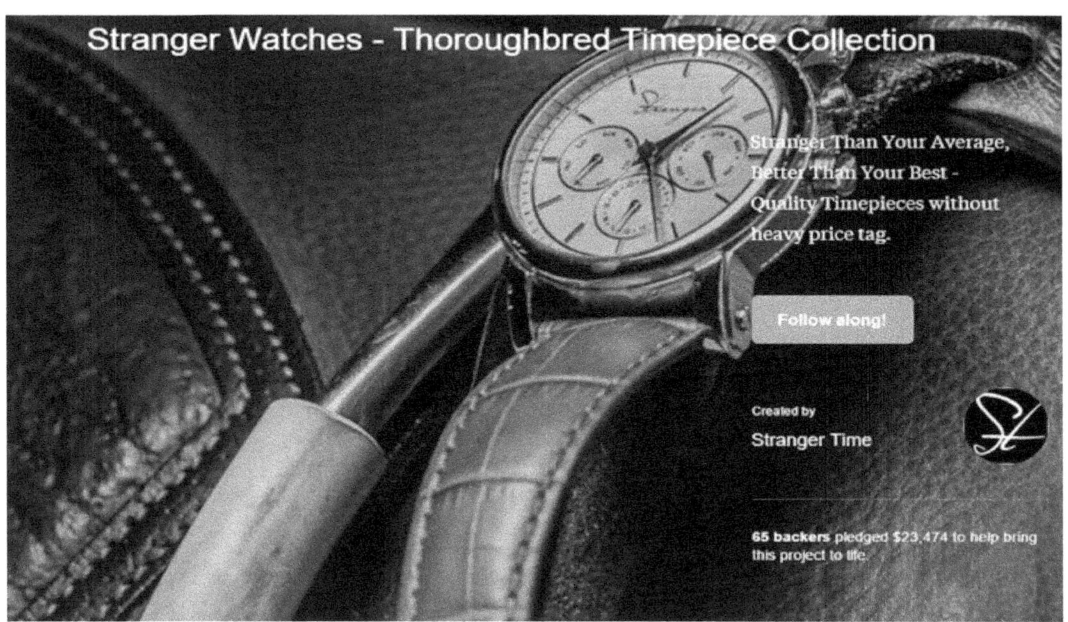
Stranger Watches - Thoroughbred Timepiece Collection
Stranger Than Your Average,
Better Than Your Best -
Quality Timepieces without
heavy price tag.
Follow along!
Created by
Stranger Time
65 backers pledged $23,474 to help bring
this project to life.

Marketing Channels: Crowdfunding

So, key summary from the Crowdfunding Campaign:
Summary

- Video
  - Appear genuine and 'human'
  - Don't hide and speak honestly
- Your Story
  - Key highlights, obstacles, objectives
- Media Coverage
  - Research other Campaigns
  - Pitch, Persist, Pitch again
- Product Highlights
- Technical Specs
- Project Timeline
- Perks
- FAQ

Marketing Channels: Crowdfunding Summary

Lessons Learned for Crowdfunding:

- Stay connected to you Backers
- Post timely Updates
- Lots of Images
- Encourage to Share
- Keep Media updated on your progress
- Celebrate Milestones

Marketing Channels: Crowdfunding Promotion

Promoting your Crowdfunding campaign is as much involving as it is marketing your entire brand. You need to start in advance, way before your campaign goes Live. You need to build a momentum. This will take a lot of creativity and persistence. At first, we analyzed the sources that covered similar campaigns to ours and we compiled a list of contacts from those avenues. We pitched them non-stop.

Social Media Marketing is a very useful tool to gain coverage for your Campaign. Broadcast on your own channels and engage others to help you spread the word. You will have to pay some of them to post about you, so choose wisely and understand their audience as well and how they would relate to you.

Forum Posts: forums can be a great source of traffic to your campaign. Some of the most popular, WatchUSeek, TimeZone, WatchFreeks, do take time to register and engage, post and write. Some of them will not let you post about your campaign straight up, so be prepared to pay. I wanted to share a quite different strategy that we decided to implement with regards to Forum Posts. It was risky but we wanted to try something different instead of just posting a nice blog post with cool images and descriptions and asking "What do you think" at the end. Here is what we plotted. We decided to post an Article in one of the more popular sections of the Forums, particularly about Crowdfunding Campaigns. What we did, is added some very blatant mistakes in our Images and Descriptions. For example, we omitted the Date window from the Dial, we said we are using 304 Grade Steel instead of the much better one 316, and added Straps that were not our size, which was obvious. As we posted this, along with everything else (our story, objectives, images), and as we had hoped this caused an uproar. Flood of nasty comments, the more educated ones provided constructive criticism pointing out some of these obvious mistakes, others were just plain laughing at us. Bottom line, the forum post caused people to Comment, Share and Talk About it. This has led to many others joining the conversation. The more comments our Forum Post was getting, the more popular it was getting and growing in rankings, moving up the charts, and attracted even more people. We did not comment or respond for about a week to build up the momentum and let the dust settle a bit (some of the commenters were very passionate about some of our "mistakes"). Then, we started engaging and replying to each comment, admitting to our "mistakes" and acknowledging that we did make those mistakes and will definitely do everything possible to fix those mistakes. Not only did this strategy make this post very popular on the forums, it also had won us some loyal fans because of the fact that we made the mistakes, admitted them and fixed them!

This strategy is not for everyone and it requires proper execution and also a thick skin (some of the comments were not so nice!), but we had to stick to the plan.

With regards to Offline strategies. Don't think that 100% of your efforts for the campaign should be Online. In fact, expand your reach and take the traditional route of promotion. Find relevant events happening in your area that you can attend. Some examples are: you can search for Networking Events on LinkedIn; specific events can be found on MeetUp or Eventbrite. Approach the organizers of these events and offer to be a sponsor in exchange for promotion of your brand and an opportunity for a quick speech in front of the audience. In exchange you can offer to conduct a drawing for a Watch for example, have people drop their business cards and then do the drawing towards the end of the night. If your watch costs you $150 to manufacture, then think of it in those terms, that it cost you $150 to advertise at this event.

When you launch your Crowdfunding campaign, you will get bombarded by offers from various quote on quote marketing companies who supposedly specialize in marketing campaigns. Bottom line, do not waste your money on that and instead focus on some strategies I mention above. Just for the sake of experiment, we have engaged with a couple of companies as such and they are pretty much worthless.

Closure

Closing Remarks

My fellow watch enthusiasts. I sincerely hope that you've enjoyed this short journey with me. I wish that I could spend much more time with you telling all the funny and not so funny stories about my experience starting and operating a watch company. The purpose of this book was to provide you with enough tool and information to prevent you from making the same mistakes that I've made as we were starting out and position you towards success as you begin your journey. Launching a watch company, or any other company is not for everyone and it is not an easy feat. At the end of the day, it is your passion for watches that will drive you, when faced with adversity and when the sales numbers are not what you've expected, it is your love for the product that will keep you going. I am always available to answer any questions or comment, or anything that I may have not covered during in this material. Feel free to reach out any time.

I am not going to wish your Luck because you are the maker of your own luck, but I would like to wish you is Patience. Have patience, the results will not be immediate, but they will come. Just be have a solid plan and relentless approach to execution and the rewards will come sooner than later. It is your Time now. Keep me posted!

Yours truly,

Jahn Karsybaev

References

Watch industry statistics. (n.d.). Retrieved April 09, 2016, from http://www.fhs.ch/eng/statistics.html

The Deloitte Swiss Watch Industry Study 2015 - Uncertain times. (n.d.). Retrieved April 09, 2016, from http://www2.deloitte.com/ch/en/pages/consumer-business/articles/swiss-watch-industry-study.html

(n.d.). Retrieved April 09, 2016, from https://www.wikipedia.org/

www.ingramcontent.com/pod-product-compliance
Ingram Content Group UK Ltd.
Pitfield, Milton Keynes, MK11 3LW, UK
UKHW051137260726
13967UKWH00010B/3104